Table Of Contents

I0409153

We all see the end results of an entrepreneur's success we see the cars and homes and exotic vacations, then we close our eyes and imagine what it would be like to be that person for a day, a week, or a month. But we don't see the struggle, or the failures that took place before the success we just think that person woke up one day and invented something that made them rich. It's not your fault it is how we were raised and conditioned to think by society. Harland David Sanders comes to mind as the biggest failure in business history, Harland was born September 9, 1890 - Henryville, Indiana, U.S. His father, Wilbert Sanders, died only five years later, forcing his mother to take work at a local tomato canning factory and sew for nearby families, often away for days at a time. In the meantime, Sanders, who was the oldest of three siblings, was forced to take care of the home and his family — this is when he started to develop his cooking skills. At the age of 10, he took his first job at a local farm. When Sanders was 12, his mother remarried and took her children to live with her new husband in the suburbs outside of Indianapolis. His relationship with his new stepfather was strained, to say the least, and the two fought often. Finally, at the age of 13, things came to a head at home and Sanders was sent back to Clark County, where the family had first lived. Sanders soon scored a job working on a farm in Greenwood, Indiana, earning $10-15 a month, plus room and board, feeding animals and performing odd jobs.

Around this time, Sanders (who'd been balancing his farm work with a full-time education) dropped out of school, only completing the sixth grade. He'd one day claim that "algebra's what drove me off."

Over the next 28 years, Sanders would take on an incredible number of different jobs across the American South. These included a brief stint in the U.S. Army (during which he was sent to Cuba), as well as working as a streetcar conductor, a railroad fireman, an insurance salesman, a secretary, a tire salesman, a ferry operator, a lawyer, and even a brief stint as a midwife (really!). Some of his career highlights included getting into a fistfight with his own client during a court case and leaving the ferry business after the construction of a nearby bridge put him out of work. As he left his youth and entered middle age, it became increasingly likely that Sanders would never achieve the success which his hard work demanded. Sanders' own family life was often tumultuous and occasionally fraught with tragedy. In 1908, he married Josephine King, a woman with whom he had three children: Margaret, Harland Jr., and Mildred. His inability to hold down a job soon proved troublesome at home, Josephine wound up leaving him for a short time — and taking the children with her — because of his career woes. They divorced in 1947. Disaster struck again when Harland Junior died at the age of 20 of complications from blood poisoning he contracted during a tonsillectomy — what was commonly regarded as a simple, routine procedure, even at the time.

According to John Ed Pearce, one of the Colonel's biographers, Sanders was afflicted with depression for a period during his adult life. Frankly, it's not difficult to see why. Finally, in 1949, he married a woman named Claudia Leddington, who he would remain with until his death in 1980. Eventually, Sanders ran a gas station in Corbin, Kentucky. To make ends meet, he began to cook and sell meals for weary travelers who stopped at the station. His food, which usually consisted of pan-fried chicken, ham, string beans, okra, and hot biscuits, garnered him something of a reputation in the region for his skills as a chef. It wasn't glamorous work, but it landed Sanders the one thing he'd never found in his life: success. It was a modest yet satisfying life for the Colonel. A few years later, he took out the gas pumps and set up his first restaurant. By this time, Sanders had begun to perfect the recipe for chicken. His winning streak grew even hotter in 1939 when he developed a method of cooking chicken via a pressure cooker which cut down on grease and preserved flavor, moisture, and texture without sacrificing cooking time. For over a decade, Sanders' restaurant prospered — but another bout of tragedy waited on the horizon. In the '50s, Colonel Sanders was struck by two blows of bad luck in rapid succession, putting the success he had finally found at great risk. The first came when the highway junction situated in front of his restaurant was moved to another location, effectively putting an end to the busy traffic which regularly passed by — and provided him with customers.

That alone would be enough to put a major dent in his business, but next came the announcement of a brand-new interstate highway that was to be built on a location that bypassed the restaurant by seven miles. It became clear that Sanders and his restaurant were about to be left in the dirt. Sensing the end was near, Sanders auctioned off the site of his restaurant in 1956, and he took a loss on the sale. With no income, he was forced to scrape by a living on his savings, the proceeds of the auction, and his Social Security check of $105 per month. After a brief and tantalizing flirtation with success, Sanders was back to square one.After the closure of his restaurant, Colonel Sanders, now devoted to his cooking, attempted a new business tactic. He traveled across the United States, visiting potential franchisee restaurants and offering them his chicken recipe in return for 4 cents on every chicken sold (he later raised it to a nickel). Sanders' first franchisee was Pete Harman, a friend in Salt Lake City, who had seen a boom in sales since beginning to serve chicken made with Sanders' method and recipe. It would not have been an easy life. Sanders would wander across the country, always on the lookout for suitable restaurants. If he found one, he'd walk inside and try to convince the owner to let him cook some chicken for the restaurant's employees. If they approved, he'd suggest cooking for the restaurant's customers for a few days. The public would then, theoretically, so enjoy this new recipe that the restaurant would enter into negotiations to begin franchising for Sanders.

It was a slow, expensive, and humiliating way to pursue business partners, and in the meantime, Sanders (and sometimes his wife) lived out of his car and ate begged meals from friends whenever he could. But it worked: By 1964, he had franchised over 600 outlets and built a company worth millions of dollars. At the age of 74, Colonel Sanders owned a thriving company with 17 employees, an office, space, and a not-inconsiderable profit margin. We still enjoy his chicken to this day his face is on the bucket. You might have heard of his chicken place KFC. *(source material: The Tragic, Real-Life Story Of Colonel Sanders BY CHRIS HEASMAN)*

The story of Colonel Sanders is one of the perfect examples of Failing forward because despite his many failures and tragic events he learned from them and continued onward.

Chapter 1: The Power of Failure

The Fear of Failure

The Fear of Failure

Fear of failure is an emotion that plagues many entrepreneurs, especially beginners in the world of business. It is a common feeling that can hold back even the most ambitious individuals from pursuing their dreams. However, in the realm of entrepreneurship, failure should not be seen as something to be avoided at all costs, but rather as a stepping stone towards success. In this subchapter, we will explore the fear of failure and how to embrace it as an entrepreneur.

One of the main reasons entrepreneurs fear failure is because they associate it with a negative outcome. They view failure as a reflection of their abilities and skills, leading to a blow to their self-esteem. However, it is crucial to understand that failure is not a reflection of who you are as a person or your capabilities as an entrepreneur. In fact, failure is a natural part of the learning process and an opportunity for growth.

Another reason for the fear of failure is the fear of financial loss. Many entrepreneurs worry about the potential consequences of a failed business venture, such as bankruptcy or financial ruin. While this fear is valid, it is essential to remember that failure is not the end of the road. Many successful entrepreneurs have experienced multiple failures before achieving their breakthrough. Failure can provide valuable lessons and insights that can help you make better decisions in the future.

To overcome the fear of failure, it is important to shift your mindset and embrace failure as a learning experience. Instead of viewing failure as a setback, see it as an opportunity for growth and improvement. Embrace the lessons learned from your failures and use them to refine your business strategies.

Furthermore, surround yourself with a supportive network of like-minded individuals who understand the challenges of entrepreneurship. Seek out mentors who have experienced failure themselves and can provide guidance and support during difficult times. Remember, you are not alone in your journey, and there are others who have faced similar obstacles and emerged stronger.

In conclusion, the fear of failure is a common emotion experienced by entrepreneurs, particularly beginners. However, it is crucial to overcome this fear and embrace failure as a necessary part of the entrepreneurial journey. Failure is not a reflection of your abilities, but an opportunity for growth and learning. Surround yourself with a supportive network, seek guidance from mentors, and shift your mindset to view failure as a stepping stone towards success. Embracing failure will not only make you a better entrepreneur but also increase your chances of achieving your goals.

Understanding the Stigma Around Failure

Understanding the Stigma Around Failure

Failure is often seen as a dirty word in the world of entrepreneurship. Society has instilled in us the belief that failure is something to be ashamed of, something to hide from others. We are conditioned to fear failure, to avoid it at all costs. But what if we were to shift our perspective? What if we were to embrace failure as a valuable learning experience?

In this subchapter, we will delve into the stigma surrounding failure, particularly in the context of starting a business. As entrepreneurs, beginners, or those who have experienced failure in their entrepreneurial journey, it is crucial to understand the negative connotations associated with failure and how it impacts our mindset and actions.

The stigma around failure can be paralyzing. It creates a fear of taking risks, of stepping out of our comfort zones. We become so focused on avoiding failure that we miss out on opportunities for growth and innovation. By understanding the stigma and the power it holds over us, we can begin to challenge it and reframe our mindset.

One of the key reasons for the stigma is our society's fixation on success. We are conditioned to celebrate success stories and idolize those who have achieved great heights. However, what we fail to recognize is that success often comes after a series of failures. Behind every successful entrepreneur, there is a trail of failed ventures and lessons learned. It is essential to realize that failure is not the opposite of success; it is an integral part of the journey towards success.

Another factor contributing to the stigma is the fear of judgment from others. We worry about what our peers, friends, and family will think if our business fails. This fear of being seen as a failure can be suffocating, preventing us from taking risks and pursuing our entrepreneurial dreams. However, it is crucial to remember that the opinions of others should not define our worth or determine our path. By reframing failure as a stepping stone towards growth, we can disarm the fear of judgment and focus on our own personal and professional development.

Understanding the stigma around failure is the first step towards embracing it as an entrepreneur. By challenging societal norms and shifting our mindset, we can unlock the true potential of failure. Failure becomes an opportunity for learning, innovation, and resilience. It becomes a stepping stone towards success rather than a roadblock.

In the upcoming chapters, we will explore practical strategies and insights from successful entrepreneurs who have embraced failure and used it as a catalyst for growth. Together, we will uncover the power of failing forward and learn how to navigate the challenges of starting a business while embracing failure as an invaluable teacher.

The Importance of Embracing Failure

The Importance of Embracing Failure

Failure is often seen as a negative outcome, something to be avoided at all costs. However, in the world of entrepreneurship, failure is not only inevitable but also essential for growth and success. In this subchapter, we will explore the importance of embracing failure and how it can be a valuable tool for entrepreneurs, especially beginners struggling with failure in starting a business.

First and foremost, failure provides invaluable lessons and insights. Every failure brings with it a wealth of knowledge and experience that cannot be gained through success alone. It forces entrepreneurs to reflect on their actions, strategies, and decisions, identifying what went wrong and how to improve. By embracing failure and learning from it, entrepreneurs can make better-informed decisions in the future, increasing their chances of success.

Moreover, failure builds resilience and perseverance. Starting a business is a challenging journey, filled with countless obstacles and setbacks. Embracing failure allows entrepreneurs to develop a strong mindset, enabling them to bounce back from disappointments and keep moving forward. It teaches them to view failure not as a sign of defeat but as an opportunity for growth and improvement. This resilience is crucial in an ever-changing business landscape, where adaptability is key to survival. a perfect example will be told in the next story.

The Next Story :

Chris's life journey was defined by numerous failures that ultimately propelled him toward success. Born into poverty and facing countless obstacles, he turned his setbacks into stepping stones, determined to create a better life for himself and his son. After realizing his passion for finance, Chris decided to pursue a career in the field. Despite lacking a formal education or prior experience, he managed to secure an unpaid internship at the prestigious brokerage firm, Dean Witter Reynolds. This opportunity, however, came with its own set of challenges. Financially strained, Chris struggled to support himself and his son, often relying on public assistance and temporary shelters. During this period, Chris faced a series of failures that tested his resolve. Despite his dedication and commitment, he struggled to make ends meet. Prospective clients were hesitant to trust a broker who was homeless and lacked a proven track record. These rejections were disheartening, but Chris refused to be deterred. Instead, he learned important lessons about perseverance and the importance of building trust and credibility in the financial industry. As Chris continued to face financial hardships, his life hit rock bottom. He and his son found themselves homeless, living on the streets of San Francisco. But even in the face of extreme adversity, Chris clung to his dreams and aspirations, refusing to let his circumstances define him.

He used the challenges as an opportunity to develop resilience, resourcefulness, and an unwavering belief in his abilities. While enduring homelessness, Chris's determination to succeed remained unshaken. He spent countless hours studying financial textbooks, analyzing stock market trends, and honing his skills. This period taught him the value of self-education and the importance of taking advantage of every opportunity to learn and grow. After a long and arduous journey, Chris finally secured a full-time position as a trainee at Dean Witter Reynolds. However, his struggles were far from over. Balancing the rigorous demands of the job with the ongoing challenges of homelessness proved to be an incredible test of his resilience. But through sheer determination and a relentless work ethic, Chris persevered, learning the invaluable lesson that success often requires immense sacrifice and perseverance. Despite facing failures and setbacks throughout his entrepreneurial journey, Chris Gardner's unwavering belief in himself led him to establish his own brokerage firm, Gardner Rich & Co. He used his experiences as a springboard for growth, understanding that failures provide opportunities for learning and growth. Chris's story serves as an inspiration to millions around the world, demonstrating that no matter how dire the circumstances may be, with determination, resilience, and a refusal to give up, success is within reach. His journey exemplifies the power of transforming failures into stepping stones, ultimately leading to triumph in the face of adversity.

It's important to remember that the true story of Chris Gardner is even more nuanced and detailed than can be fully captured here. His autobiography, "The Pursuit of Happyness," provides a more comprehensive account of his experiences, including his failures and the lessons he learned along the way.

Failure also encourages innovation and creativity. When entrepreneurs are not afraid of failing, they are more inclined to take risks and think outside the box. They are not limited by the fear of making mistakes or the pressure to conform to conventional norms. Embracing failure allows entrepreneurs to push boundaries, explore new ideas, and find unique solutions to problems. Some of the greatest innovations and breakthroughs have come as a result of failures, demonstrating the immense power of embracing failure as an entrepreneur.

Lastly, failure builds character and humility. It humbles entrepreneurs, reminding them that success is not guaranteed, and that they are not infallible. It encourages them to seek help, collaborate with others, and learn from those who have experienced similar failures. This humility fosters personal and professional growth, allowing entrepreneurs to develop a greater understanding of themselves and their strengths and weaknesses.

Let's talk about Sara. Sara's entrepreneurial journey began when she came up with the idea for a unique woman's undergarment. Despite having no background in fashion or business, she was determined to bring her innovative undergarment concept to life. However, her initial attempts to find manufacturers for her product were met with countless rejections. Sara persevered through these setbacks, maintaining her belief in her idea and refusing to give up. Undeterred by the rejections, Sara decided to take matters into her own hands. She invested her life savings and worked tirelessly to create a prototype. Armed with her product, she set out to demonstrate its potential to retailers. One of her most memorable moments came when she persuaded a buyer from a major department store to give her a chance. Sara found herself pitching her product by wearing the prototype herself and highlighting its unique benefits. Her determination and passion ultimately convinced the buyer, and Spanx secured a place on the store's shelves. However, even after this initial success, challenges persisted. Sara faced numerous obstacles in scaling up her business and building brand recognition. Yet, she remained focused and committed to her vision. She continuously sought feedback from customers, making adjustments to improve the product and better meet their needs. Sara's ability to learn from her failures and adapt to the market allowed Spanx to gain popularity and become a household name. Throughout her entrepreneurial journey, Sara Blakely maintained a humble approach.

She openly shares her failures and the lessons she learned from them.

Blakely believes in the importance of taking risks, embracing failure as an opportunity for growth, and maintaining a positive mindset. Her humility has contributed to her success and has allowed her to connect with customers on a personal level. Today, Spanx is a globally recognized brand, and Sara Blakely is not only a successful entrepreneur but also a philanthropist and advocate for women's empowerment. She has used her success to support and inspire other aspiring entrepreneurs, particularly women, encouraging them to embrace failure, be resilient, and pursue their dreams. Sara Blakely's story is a testament to the power of perseverance, humility, and unwavering belief in one's ideas. Her journey reminds us that failures and rejections can be transformative moments that pave the way for success and that embracing those failures with humility and determination can lead to extraordinary achievements.

In conclusion, failure should not be feared or avoided but embraced as an essential part of the entrepreneurial journey. It provides valuable lessons, builds resilience and perseverance, encourages innovation and creativity, and fosters character and humility. By embracing failure, entrepreneurs can turn setbacks into stepping stones towards success. So, let go of the fear of failure, embrace it as a learning opportunity, and fail forward towards your entrepreneurial dreams.

Chapter 2: Building a Resilient Mindset

Cultivating a Growth Mindset

Cultivating a Growth Mindset

In the journey of entrepreneurship, failure is an inevitable part of the process. As entrepreneurs, beginners often face numerous challenges and setbacks when starting a business. However, it is crucial to understand that failure is not the end but a stepping stone towards success. To navigate these obstacles successfully, it is essential to cultivate a growth mindset.

A growth mindset is a powerful tool that allows entrepreneurs to embrace failure, learn from it, and continually improve. It is the belief that abilities and intelligence can be developed through dedication, hard work, and perseverance. Entrepreneurs with a growth mindset see failure as an opportunity for growth and development rather than a setback.

The first step in cultivating a growth mindset is to reframe how you perceive failure. Instead of viewing failure as a personal reflection of your abilities, see it as a valuable learning experience. Understand that every setback provides a chance to gain new insights, refine your strategies, and ultimately improve your chances of success.

Embracing failure also means taking risks and stepping out of your comfort zone. Many entrepreneurs fear failure and avoid taking risks. However, without taking calculated risks, it is impossible to achieve significant growth and success. By embracing failure, you are willing to learn from your mistakes, adapt, and innovate. Stop me if you have heard these excuses or have used them

"I don't have enough time": This excuse suggests that individuals believe they are too busy or overwhelmed to take on new challenges or risks.

"I'm not ready yet": This excuse reflects a mindset of waiting for the perfect moment or feeling fully prepared before taking action. People may convince themselves that they need more knowledge, skills, or experience before attempting something new, using this as a reason to avoid potential mistakes.

"It's too risky": This excuse emphasizes the fear of negative consequences and potential failure. People may perceive the potential risks associated with making a mistake as too high and decide to play it safe by not taking any action at all.

"I can't afford to make a mistake": This excuse often arises in situations involving financial or career decisions. Individuals may fear that a mistake could lead to significant financial losses, missed opportunities, or setbacks in their professional advancement.

Consequently, they choose to avoid making decisions altogether. "What will others think?": The fear of judgment and criticism from others can be a powerful excuse. People may worry about how their mistakes will be perceived by friends, family, colleagues, or society at large. This concern about the opinions of others can hold them back from taking risks or pursuing their goals.

"I'm not good enough": This excuse is rooted in self-doubt and a lack of confidence. Individuals may believe that they are not capable or talented enough to succeed, leading them to avoid situations where mistakes could potentially highlight their perceived inadequacies.

"It's not worth the effort": This excuse suggests that individuals do not see the potential benefits or rewards as significant enough to justify the risk of making mistakes. They may weigh the potential challenges and setbacks against the perceived benefits and decide that it is not worth the effort to try. It is important to recognize that these excuses often stem from fear, self-doubt, and a desire to avoid discomfort. Overcoming these excuses requires embracing a growth mindset, understanding that mistakes are part of the learning process, and acknowledging that they can lead to personal growth and improvement.

One effective way to cultivate a growth mindset is through continuous learning and self-improvement. Seek out opportunities to expand your knowledge, whether through reading books, attending workshops, or networking with other entrepreneurs. Embrace feedback and surround yourself with mentors who can provide guidance and support.

Another essential aspect of a growth mindset is perseverance. Entrepreneurship is a challenging journey, and setbacks are bound to occur. However, a growth mindset encourages entrepreneurs to persevere through adversity. Use failure as fuel to motivate yourself, and keep pushing forward despite the obstacles you may face.

Lastly, remember that failure is NOT a reflection of your worth or potential. It is merely a temporary setback on the path to success. Cultivating a growth mindset allows you to bounce back from failure stronger and more resilient than before.

In conclusion, cultivating a growth mindset is vital for entrepreneurs, especially beginners who often face failure in starting a business. By reframing how you perceive failure, embracing risks, continuously learning, persevering, and understanding that failure does not define you, you can harness the power of a growth mindset to propel yourself towards success. Embrace failure as an opportunity for growth, and you will be well on your way to becoming a resilient and successful entrepreneur.

Overcoming the Fear of Judgment

Overcoming the Fear of Judgment

One of the biggest obstacles that entrepreneurs, especially beginners, face when starting a business is the fear of judgment. The fear of what others might think or say about their ideas, their abilities, and their potential for success can be paralyzing. However, it is essential to understand that failure is a natural part of the entrepreneurial journey, and overcoming the fear of judgment is crucial for growth and success.

Firstly, it is important to realize that everyone faces judgment, regardless of their entrepreneurial endeavors. Whether you succeed or fail, there will always be people who criticize and doubt your decisions. Understanding this universal truth is the first step towards overcoming the fear of judgment. Embrace the fact that you cannot please everyone, and focus on your own goals and vision.

Secondly, surround yourself with a supportive network of like-minded individuals who understand the challenges and risks involved in starting a business. It would be ideal if the support comes from your family, But I found that family can know you yet not *understand* you at the same time So expect your family to be your harshest critics before they become your biggest supporters. Seek out mentors, join entrepreneur communities, and attend networking events to connect with people who have experienced similar struggles. Having a supportive network can provide you with the encouragement and guidance you need to overcome the fear of judgment. Know where they hang out When I was performing Magic shows I would shop at TANNENS MAGIC STORE in Manhattan, and I would make sure I would get there on Saturday afternoon at least an hour and a half before closing. Why you ask because that's when all the old school Magicians would show up and I'm talking these are the guys who made a living touring and performing long before the likes of David Copperfield, Chris Angel, etc. and they would leave the store when it closed and go around the corner to a pizza shop and for three hours, I learned techniques and sleights lost that was lost for decades because these guys made them up and perfected them in real-world settings and they would mentor anyone who ventured into the pizzeria and demonstrate skills, you just couldn't walk up to these legends and ask them to learn their secrets without proving you were not a looky-loo.

This is probably what you are going to have to do to find your mentor so seek them out they are waiting for you.

Another effective strategy is to shift your mindset towards failure. Instead of viewing failure as something to be avoided at all costs, embrace it as a valuable learning experience. Understand that failure is inevitable on the path to success and that it is an opportunity to grow and improve. By reframing failure in this way, you can overcome the fear of judgment and take calculated risks without the fear of what others might say.

Additionally, practice self-compassion and self-belief. Remind yourself that you are capable of achieving your goals and that setbacks are a part of the journey. Celebrate your wins, no matter how small, and learn from your failures. By building self-confidence and self-trust, you can overcome the fear of judgment and stay focused on your entrepreneurial journey.

In conclusion, the fear of judgment is a common hurdle faced by entrepreneurs, especially those starting a business. However, it is important to remember that failure is a normal part of the journey. Surround yourself with supportive individuals, shift your mindset towards failure, and practice self-compassion. By embracing failure and overcoming the fear of judgment, you can navigate the challenges of entrepreneurship and ultimately find success.

Developing Emotional Resilience

Developing Emotional Resilience

Failure is an inevitable part of starting a business. As an entrepreneur, you will face numerous setbacks, obstacles, and disappointments along the way. However, it is your ability to bounce back from these failures that will determine your success in the long run. Developing emotional resilience is crucial for overcoming the challenges you will face as a beginner entrepreneur.

Emotional resilience is the ability to adapt and recover from adversity, setbacks, and failure. It involves maintaining a positive mindset, managing stress, and staying motivated despite the difficulties that arise. This subchapter will explore strategies and techniques to help you build emotional resilience and embrace failure as an essential stepping stone towards success.

One of the first steps in developing emotional resilience is shifting your mindset towards failure. Instead of viewing failure as something to be ashamed of or avoided, see it as an opportunity for growth and learning. Understand that failures are not personal flaws or indicators of incompetence, but rather valuable lessons that can guide you towards improvement.

Another important aspect of emotional resilience is managing stress effectively. Starting a business can be overwhelming, and stress is bound to arise. Learning stress management techniques, such as deep breathing exercises, meditation, or even physical activities like yoga or running, can help you stay calm and focused during challenging times.

Additionally, building a support system is crucial for entrepreneurs facing failure. Surround yourself with like-minded individuals who understand and support your entrepreneurial journey. Seek advice and mentorship from experienced entrepreneurs who have been through similar failures and can provide guidance and encouragement. Remember, you are not alone in this journey, and having a network of support can make a significant difference in building emotional resilience.

Lastly, staying motivated and maintaining a positive mindset is essential for overcoming failure. Celebrate small wins along the way, no matter how insignificant they may seem. Develop a habit of gratitude and practice positive affirmations to keep your spirits high during tough times.

In conclusion, developing emotional resilience is crucial for entrepreneurs facing failure in starting a business. By shifting your mindset, managing stress effectively, building a support system, and staying motivated, you can overcome the challenges and embrace failure as a valuable learning opportunity. Remember, failure is not the end; it is the beginning of a new and better version of yourself as an entrepreneur. Embrace failure, learn from it, and keep moving forward towards your ultimate success.

Chapter 3: Learning from Failure

Embracing a Growth Mindset in Failure

Embracing a Growth Mindset in Failure

Failure is an inevitable part of the entrepreneurial journey, especially when starting a business. It is essential for entrepreneurs, beginners, and those facing failures in starting a business to embrace a growth mindset. By adopting this mindset, one can transform failures into valuable learning experiences and pave the way for future success.

A growth mindset is the belief that abilities and intelligence can be developed through dedication, effort, and a willingness to learn. It is the understanding that failure is not a reflection of one's worth or potential but rather an opportunity for growth and improvement. Entrepreneurs must internalize this mindset to navigate the challenges and setbacks they encounter on their entrepreneurial path.

One of the key aspects of embracing a growth mindset is reframing failure as a stepping stone to success. Instead of viewing failure as a roadblock or a reason to give up, entrepreneurs should see it as a valuable lesson. Each failure provides an opportunity to learn, adapt, and refine their strategies. By embracing failure, entrepreneurs can identify their weaknesses, make necessary adjustments, and ultimately increase their chances of success.

Another crucial element of a growth mindset is the willingness to take risks and step outside of one's comfort zone. Entrepreneurs who fear failure often hesitate to pursue innovative ideas or take bold actions. However, by embracing a growth mindset, entrepreneurs can overcome this fear and embrace failure as an integral part of the learning process. Taking calculated risks and being open to failure allows entrepreneurs to push boundaries, explore new opportunities, and ultimately achieve breakthroughs in their business.

Moreover, a growth mindset enables entrepreneurs to approach failure with resilience and perseverance. Instead of dwelling on past failures, entrepreneurs with a growth mindset bounce back quickly, evaluate their mistakes, and develop new strategies. They understand that failure is not permanent and that setbacks are merely temporary roadblocks on the path to success.

In conclusion, embracing a growth mindset in failure is crucial for entrepreneurs, beginners, and those facing failures in starting a business. By reframing failure as an opportunity for growth, taking calculated risks, and approaching setbacks with resilience, entrepreneurs can turn failures into valuable learning experiences. Failure becomes a stepping stone towards success rather than an obstacle to overcome. By embracing a growth mindset, entrepreneurs can navigate the challenges of starting a business with confidence and determination.

Extracting Valuable Lessons from Mistakes

Extracting Valuable Lessons from Mistakes

Mistakes are an inevitable part of the entrepreneurial journey, especially for beginners in the world of business. However, what separates successful entrepreneurs from the rest is their ability to extract valuable lessons from these mistakes. In this subchapter, we will explore the importance of learning from failures and how to turn them into stepping stones on your path to success.

One of the key lessons to learn from mistakes is the power of resilience. As an entrepreneur, you will face numerous challenges and setbacks. It is crucial to embrace failure as an opportunity to grow and persevere through tough times. By developing a resilient mindset, you can bounce back stronger, armed with the knowledge gained from your mistakes.

Another valuable lesson to extract from failures is the importance of analyzing and understanding the root causes of your mistakes. Take the time to reflect on what went wrong and why. By delving deeper into the reasons behind your failures, you can identify patterns or weaknesses that need to be addressed. This self-reflection will enable you to make more informed decisions and avoid repeating similar mistakes in the future.

Furthermore, mistakes provide invaluable insights into market dynamics and customer preferences. Every failure presents an opportunity to gather data and feedback that can guide your future business strategies. Analyze customer reactions, conduct post-mortems, and seek feedback from trusted sources to gain a comprehensive understanding of what works and what doesn't. This knowledge will prove to be instrumental in refining your business model and enhancing your product or service offerings.

Additionally, mistakes offer a chance for personal growth and development. As an entrepreneur, you are constantly learning and evolving. Failing forward allows you to build resilience, develop problem-solving skills, and cultivate emotional intelligence. Embrace failures as opportunities for self-improvement and use them to strengthen your entrepreneurial skillset.

Lastly, remember that mistakes are not indicative of failure but rather a stepping stone towards success. Many renowned entrepreneurs have faced numerous failures before achieving greatness. Embrace failure as a natural part of the entrepreneurial journey and approach it with a growth mindset. Learn from your mistakes, adapt, and keep moving forward.

In conclusion, the subchapter "Extracting Valuable Lessons from Mistakes" emphasizes the importance of learning from failures for entrepreneurs, especially those starting their own businesses. By embracing failure, developing resilience, analyzing mistakes, gathering insights, fostering personal growth, and maintaining a growth mindset, entrepreneurs can transform their mistakes into invaluable lessons that propel them towards success. Remember, failure is not the end but rather a stepping stone on your path to entrepreneurial greatness.

The Role of Reflection in Failure

The Role of Reflection in Failure

Failure is often seen as a negative outcome, especially in the world of entrepreneurship. Many beginners fear failure and view it as a setback or a sign of incompetence. However, what if I told you that failure can actually be a valuable tool for growth and success? It all comes down to the role of reflection in failure.

Reflection is the process of looking back on your experiences, analyzing them, and extracting lessons from them. When it comes to failure, reflection is crucial because it allows us to understand what went wrong, why it went wrong, and how we can avoid making the same mistakes in the future.

For entrepreneurs, failure in starting a business is not uncommon. In fact, it is often considered a rite of passage. Reflecting on these failures can provide invaluable insights that can propel your entrepreneurial journey forward.

One of the main reasons reflection is so important in failure is because it helps us gain a deeper understanding of ourselves and our businesses. By taking the time to reflect on our failures, we can identify our strengths and weaknesses, as well as the areas where we need to improve. This self-awareness is essential for growth and personal development.

Reflection also helps us identify patterns and trends in our failures. Are there certain mistakes that keep popping up? Are there specific areas of our business that consistently underperform? By recognizing these patterns, we can make informed decisions and take proactive measures to address them.Let's imagine a scenario where a person named Alex aspires to be a successful entrepreneur. They have attempted several business ventures in the past but have faced multiple failures. Alex decides to reflect on their past mistakes to identify any recurring patterns or trends that may have contributed to their lack of success. As Alex reflects on their failures, they notice a pattern of insufficient market research and a lack of understanding of target customers. In multiple instances, they rushed into launching their products or services without thoroughly understanding the needs and preferences of their target audience. This led to products that failed to resonate with customers or solve their problems effectively. Additionally, Alex realizes that they often struggled with effective communication and marketing strategies. They consistently fell short in effectively conveying the unique value proposition of their offerings to potential customers. This lack of clarity and persuasive messaging hindered their ability to attract and retain customers. Moreover, Alex notices a recurring pattern of not properly managing their finances. In multiple ventures, they struggled with budgeting, cash flow management, and making informed financial decisions.

This pattern of financial mismanagement had a negative impact on their overall business operations and sustainability. By recognizing these patterns and trends in their failures, Alex gains valuable insights. They understand the specific areas where they need to improve and develop their skills. Armed with this knowledge, Alex can now take targeted actions to address these weaknesses, such as conducting thorough market research, enhancing their communication and marketing strategies, and seeking financial management guidance. Alex also realizes the importance of learning from successful entrepreneurs who have expertise in these areas. They actively seek out mentors or industry experts who can provide guidance and support to fill the knowledge gaps and help avoid repeating the same mistakes. Through reflection, Alex has gained a clearer understanding of the recurring patterns and trends in their failures. This self-awareness enables them to make informed decisions, take corrective actions, and increase their chances of success in future entrepreneurial endeavors.

In addition, reflection allows us to learn from the failures of others. By studying case studies and success stories, we can gain valuable insights and avoid repeating the same mistakes. This is particularly important for beginners who may not have as much firsthand experience in entrepreneurship.

Lastly, reflection on failure helps us develop resilience and a growth mindset. It teaches us to view failure as a stepping stone rather than an endpoint. By reframing failure as an opportunity to learn and improve, we become more resilient and better equipped to navigate the challenges of entrepreneurship.

In conclusion, reflection plays a vital role in failure, especially in the context of starting a business. It helps us gain self-awareness, identify patterns, learn from the experiences of others, and develop resilience. Embracing failure and using it as a catalyst for growth is a mindset that every entrepreneur, especially beginners, should adopt. So, the next time you face failure, take a moment to reflect and turn it into a stepping stone on your path to success.

Chapter 4: Failure as a Catalyst for Success

Embracing Failure as a Stepping Stone

Embracing Failure as a Stepping Stone

Failure is an inevitable part of the entrepreneurial journey. As entrepreneurs, beginners or seasoned, we are bound to encounter setbacks and obstacles along the way. However, what sets successful entrepreneurs apart is their ability to embrace failure as a stepping stone towards growth and success.

In the subchapter "Embracing Failure as a Stepping Stone" of the book "Fail Forward: Embracing Failure as an Entrepreneur," we delve into the crucial mindset shift required to turn failures into opportunities for learning and progress. This subchapter specifically addresses the niche of failure in starting a business, providing valuable insights and practical strategies to navigate this challenging phase.

Starting a business is a daunting endeavor, filled with uncertainties and risks. Many entrepreneurs face the fear of failure, which often hinders their progress and holds them back from taking necessary risks. However, it is essential to understand that failure is not the opposite of success; it is a vital component of the journey towards it.

We begin by debunking the myth that failure equals defeat. Instead, we encourage entrepreneurs to embrace failure as a valuable teacher. Each failure offers unique lessons and insights that can be applied to future endeavors. By reframing failure as an opportunity for growth, entrepreneurs can develop resilience and adaptability, essential qualities for long-term success.

Furthermore, we explore practical strategies to transform failure into a stepping stone. We delve into the importance of self-reflection and self-awareness, encouraging entrepreneurs to analyze their failures objectively. This process allows individuals to identify patterns, weaknesses, and areas for improvement, setting the stage for personal and professional growth.

Additionally, we provide guidance on building a support system and seeking mentorship. Surrounding oneself with like-minded individuals who have experienced similar failures can provide invaluable advice, encouragement, and inspiration. Learning from the mistakes and successes of others can accelerate the journey to success.

Throughout this subchapter, we share real-life stories of renowned entrepreneurs who faced significant failures in their early ventures. These stories highlight the resilience and determination required to bounce back from failure and ultimately achieve great success. By witnessing the journeys of others, entrepreneurs can gain perspective and realize that failure is merely a temporary setback, not a roadblock.

In conclusion, "Embracing Failure as a Stepping Stone" is an essential subchapter in "Fail Forward: Embracing Failure as an Entrepreneur." It addresses the fears and challenges specifically associated with failure in starting a business. By adopting the right mindset, learning from failures, and seeking support, entrepreneurs can transform setbacks into stepping stones, propelling themselves towards long-term success.

The Role of Failure in Innovation

The Role of Failure in Innovation

Innovation is often associated with success, breakthroughs, and game-changing ideas. However, what many entrepreneurs fail to realize is that failure plays a crucial role in the process of innovation. In fact, failure is not only inevitable but also essential for true innovation to take place. This subchapter aims to shed light on the significance of failure in the entrepreneurial journey, particularly in the context of starting a business.

For entrepreneurs, failure is often seen as a setback or a roadblock that hinders progress. However, it is through failure that valuable lessons are learned, new perspectives are gained, and innovative ideas are born. Failure provides entrepreneurs with the opportunity to reassess their strategies, identify weaknesses, and make the necessary adjustments to achieve success.

One of the key reasons why failure is vital in innovation is that it encourages entrepreneurs to step out of their comfort zones. When things are going smoothly, there is little incentive to explore new ideas or take risks. Failure forces entrepreneurs to think outside the box, to experiment with different approaches, and to challenge the status quo. It is in these moments of failure that groundbreaking innovations are often discovered.

Moreover, failure fosters resilience and perseverance in entrepreneurs. Starting a business is a daunting task, and setbacks are bound to happen. However, it is through failure that entrepreneurs develop the strength to bounce back, learn from their mistakes, and keep pushing forward. Failure teaches entrepreneurs to embrace uncertainty and adapt to unexpected challenges, ultimately making them more resilient and better equipped to innovate.

Furthermore, failure cultivates a culture of learning and continuous improvement. Each failure provides an opportunity to analyze what went wrong, why it happened, and how it can be prevented in the future. By embracing failure and encouraging a growth mindset, entrepreneurs can create an environment that values learning from mistakes and using that knowledge to fuel innovation.

In conclusion, failure is an integral part of the entrepreneurial journey, especially when starting a business. Rather than viewing failure as a setback, entrepreneurs should embrace it as a stepping stone to innovation. By recognizing the role of failure in the process of innovation, entrepreneurs can learn from their mistakes, develop resilience, and create a culture of continuous improvement. Embracing failure and viewing it as a necessary part of the journey will ultimately lead to greater success and groundbreaking innovations.

Transforming Failures into Opportunities

Subchapter: Transforming Failures into Opportunities

Introduction:
In the realm of entrepreneurship, failure is often seen as a setback, a stumbling block on the path to success. However, what if we told you that failure could be the catalyst for growth, innovation, and ultimately, success? In this subchapter, we explore the concept of transforming failures into opportunities, providing valuable insights and strategies for entrepreneurs, especially beginners, who have encountered failure in starting their businesses. So, buckle up and get ready to embrace failure as a stepping stone to greatness.

1. Embracing a Growth Mindset:
The first step in transforming failures into opportunities is adopting a growth mindset. Understand that failure is not a reflection of your worth or abilities as an entrepreneur, but rather an opportunity to learn, evolve, and improve.

Embrace failure as a natural part of the entrepreneurial journey and shift your perspective towards embracing the lessons it offers.

2. Analyzing Failure:

To effectively transform failures into opportunities, entrepreneurs must critically analyze their failures. Identify the root causes, examine the decisions made, and evaluate the external factors that contributed to the failure. This introspection will help you extract valuable insights and make informed decisions moving forward.

3. Learning from Mistakes:

Failure is not the end; it is merely a detour on the path to success. Learn from your mistakes and use them as building blocks for future endeavors. Failures provide invaluable lessons that can lead to innovative solutions, revised strategies, and enhanced business models. Embrace these lessons and apply them to your next venture.

4. Leveraging Failure for Growth:

Failure often unveils hidden opportunities. Use your failures as a launching pad for growth and transformation. Identify the areas where you fell short and explore how you can turn them into strengths. Seek feedback from mentors, industry experts, and customers to gain new perspectives and refine your approach.

5. Cultivating Resilience:

Resilience is key to transforming failures into opportunities. Entrepreneurs must develop the ability to bounce back from setbacks, adapt to changing circumstances, and persevere in the face of challenges. Build a support network of like-minded individuals who can provide encouragement, guidance, and inspiration during tough times.

Conclusion:

Transforming failures into opportunities is a mindset shift that empowers entrepreneurs to rise above setbacks and thrive. By embracing failure, analyzing mistakes, and leveraging lessons, entrepreneurs can not only learn from their failures but also turn them into stepping stones for success. Remember, failure is not the opposite of success; it is an essential part of the journey towards achieving greatness. So, embrace failure, learn from it, and let it propel you towards entrepreneurial excellence.

Here are a few examples.

Elon Musk: Known for his ventures such as Tesla, SpaceX, and SolarCity, Elon Musk has experienced numerous setbacks and failures throughout his career. From SpaceX's initial launch failures to Tesla's production challenges, Musk has openly acknowledged his mistakes and shortcomings. These experiences have taught him humility, leading him to make necessary adjustments and improvements while staying focused on his long-term goals.

Oprah Winfrey: As one of the most successful media moguls in the world, Oprah Winfrey faced numerous obstacles throughout her career. She encountered failure early on, including being fired from her first television job. However, Winfrey learned valuable lessons from those experiences and remained committed to personal growth and learning from her mistakes. Her humility and ability to empathize with others have been key factors in her success.

Richard Branson: The founder of Virgin Group, Richard Branson, has had his fair share of failures along the way. From failed business ventures to public missteps, Branson has openly admitted his mistakes and the lessons learned from them. He has emphasized the importance of humility and resilience in facing challenges and remaining open to continuous learning.

Sara Blakely: The founder of Spanx, Sara Blakely faced numerous rejections before finding success. She encountered countless failures while pitching her innovative undergarment concept to manufacturers and investors.

Despite the setbacks, Blakely remained persistent and used the failures as opportunities to refine her product and pitch. Her humble approach and willingness to learn from failure eventually led to the creation of a billion-dollar company.

Steve Jobs: Co-founder of Apple Inc., Steve Jobs experienced significant failures throughout his career, including being ousted from the company he helped build. However, Jobs's experiences taught him valuable lessons in humility and resilience. His subsequent return to Apple marked a transformative period in his life, where he emphasized the importance of teamwork, collaboration, and personal growth.

Chapter 5: Overcoming Fear and Taking Action

Identifying and Overcoming Fear of Failure

Identifying and Overcoming Fear of Failure

As entrepreneurs, beginners in the daunting world of business, it is not uncommon to experience a fear of failure. The fear of failure can be paralyzing, preventing us from taking risks, pursuing our dreams, and ultimately achieving success. However, by understanding and confronting this fear head-on, we can transform it into a powerful tool for growth and progress.

The first step in overcoming the fear of failure is to identify its presence in our lives. Often, this fear manifests itself as self-doubt, procrastination, or a reluctance to step out of our comfort zones. It is important to recognize that failure is a natural part of the entrepreneurial journey, and it should not define our self-worth or inhibit our progress. By acknowledging our fear, we can begin to take proactive steps toward conquering it.

One effective strategy for overcoming the fear of failure is to shift our mindset and view failure as a valuable learning experience. Instead of dreading failure, we can reframe it as an opportunity for growth and improvement. By embracing failure as a stepping stone towards success, we can develop resilience, perseverance, and a willingness to take calculated risks. Accepting failure as an integral part of the entrepreneurial process allows us to learn from our mistakes and adapt our strategies accordingly.

Another crucial aspect of overcoming the fear of failure is to surround ourselves with a supportive network. By connecting with fellow entrepreneurs who have faced similar challenges, we can gain valuable insights and advice. Sharing our fears and vulnerabilities with like-minded individuals not only alleviates the burden but also provides a sense of camaraderie. Additionally, seeking guidance from mentors who have experienced both success and failure can offer invaluable wisdom and encouragement.

Moreover, it is essential to develop a growth mindset, which emphasizes the belief that our abilities and intelligence can be cultivated through dedication and hard work. By acknowledging that failure is not a reflection of our inherent abilities but rather a temporary setback, we can bounce back stronger and more determined. Embracing a growth mindset allows us to view failure as a necessary step towards success, fostering resilience and perseverance.

In conclusion, identifying and overcoming the fear of failure is crucial for entrepreneurs, especially beginners facing the challenges of starting a business. By recognizing the presence of fear, reframing failure as a learning opportunity, building a supportive network, and adopting a growth mindset, we can transform our fear into a powerful catalyst for growth and success. Embrace failure as an entrepreneur, and you will discover that it is not an obstacle but a stepping stone towards achieving your dreams.

Taking the First Step Towards Entrepreneurship

Taking the First Step Towards Entrepreneurship

Starting a business can be an exhilarating and rewarding journey, but it can also be filled with challenges and failures. For entrepreneurs, beginners who are facing failure in starting a business, it is crucial to understand that failure is an inevitable part of the process. In this subchapter, we will delve into the importance of taking the first step towards entrepreneurship and how embracing failure can lead to success.

One of the most significant hurdles for aspiring entrepreneurs is the fear of failure. Many individuals hesitate to take the plunge because they are afraid of the unknown and the possibility of not achieving their desired outcome.

However, it is essential to shift this mindset and view failure as a stepping stone towards success. Each failure brings valuable lessons and insights that can guide you towards making better decisions in the future.

Taking the first step towards entrepreneurship requires a strong belief in yourself and your ideas. It is important to have a clear vision and a solid plan in place. However, it is equally important to understand that your initial plan may not work out as expected. This is where the willingness to adapt and learn from failure becomes crucial. By embracing failure, you can pivot and make necessary adjustments to your business strategy, ultimately increasing your chances of success.

Another crucial aspect of taking the first step towards entrepreneurship is building a strong support system. Surround yourself with like-minded individuals who have experienced failure and overcome it. Seek guidance from mentors and join networking groups where you can share your experiences and learn from others. These connections can provide valuable insights, advice, and emotional support during challenging times.

Furthermore, it is important to remember that failure is not the end, but rather a stepping stone towards growth. Embrace failure as an opportunity to learn, innovate, and improve. Analyze your failures, identify the reasons behind them, and implement changes accordingly. Celebrate small wins along the way and stay motivated even when faced with setbacks.

In conclusion, taking the first step towards entrepreneurship requires courage, resilience, and a willingness to embrace failure. As an entrepreneur, beginner experiencing failure in starting a business, it is essential to understand that failure is not a sign of weakness, but rather an opportunity for growth. By shifting your mindset and learning from failures, you can navigate the challenges of entrepreneurship more effectively and increase your chances of long-term success. Remember, failure is not the end, but a stepping stone towards achieving your entrepreneurial dreams.

Building Confidence in the Face of Failure

Failure is an inevitable part of the entrepreneurial journey, especially when starting a business. Many entrepreneurs, beginners in particular, often find themselves overwhelmed by the fear of failure. However, it is important to understand that failure is not something to be feared, but rather embraced as a stepping stone towards success. In this subchapter, we will explore strategies to help entrepreneurs build confidence in the face of failure Meet Sarah, an aspiring writer who has faced numerous rejections for her manuscripts. Despite her passion for writing, the repeated failures have shaken her confidence. However, Sarah is determined to overcome her self-doubt and build her confidence in the face of failure. Embracing a Growth Mindset: Sarah understands that failure is a natural part of the learning process. She shifts her perspective and embraces a growth mindset, viewing each rejection as an opportunity for growth and improvement. She believes that her writing skills can be honed through continuous learning and practice. Learning from Rejections: Instead of letting rejections discourage her, Sarah analyzes the feedback she receives from publishers and editors. She looks for patterns and common themes in the feedback, aiming to identify areas of improvement. Sarah recognizes that feedback, even when critical, is valuable for her growth as a writer. Celebrating Small Wins: Sarah acknowledges her progress and celebrates small wins along the way.

She sets achievable goals, such as completing a certain number of writing exercises or receiving constructive feedback from a writing group. Celebrating these milestones boosts her confidence and motivates her to keep pushing forward. Seeking Support and Encouragement: Sarah surrounds herself with a supportive network of fellow writers and mentors. She joins writing communities, attends workshops, and participates in critique groups. Through these interactions, she receives constructive feedback, encouragement, and valuable insights from others who have faced similar challenges. Practicing Self-Compassion: Sarah acknowledges that failure is a part of the creative process. She practices self-compassion by reminding herself that setbacks and rejections are not a reflection of her worth as a writer or as a person. She treats herself with kindness and understanding, cultivating a positive and nurturing mindset. Continuing Education and Skill Development: Sarah invests in her writing education by attending writing courses, reading books on craft, and exploring new writing techniques. She understands that continuous learning and skill development are crucial for her growth as a writer. By acquiring new knowledge and refining her craft, Sarah boosts her confidence in her abilities. Taking Calculated Risks: Sarah pushes herself to step outside her comfort zone and take calculated risks. She submits her work to different publishers, explores different genres, or experiments with new writing styles. By embracing new challenges, Sarah builds resilience and expands her creative horizons.

Over time, Sarah's confidence as a writer grows as she applies these strategies. She learns to view failure as an opportunity for growth, embraces her journey as a writer, and gains the confidence to persevere in the face of setbacks. Sarah's resilience, determination, and self-belief become the foundation for her continued growth and success as a writer.

The first step in building confidence is to reframe your perception of failure. Rather than viewing failure as a negative outcome, see it as a valuable learning experience. Understand that every successful entrepreneur has faced failures along the way, and it is these failures that have helped them grow and improve. By reframing failure in this way, you can begin to see it as an opportunity for growth and development.

Another strategy to build confidence is to adopt a growth mindset. Embrace the belief that your abilities and intelligence can be developed through dedication and hard work. With a growth mindset, you will view failure as a temporary setback rather than a reflection of your abilities. This mindset allows you to bounce back from failure, learn from your mistakes, and approach future challenges with renewed determination.

Surrounding yourself with a support network is crucial for building confidence in the face of failure. Connect with other entrepreneurs who have experienced similar challenges and setbacks. Share your stories and learn from each other's experiences. Having a supportive community can provide encouragement, advice, and perspective when you need it the most.

Taking small steps and celebrating your achievements along the way can also help boost your confidence. Break down your goals into manageable tasks and focus on accomplishing them one at a time. Each small success will contribute to your overall confidence and motivate you to keep moving forward, even in the face of failure.

Lastly, remember to practice self-compassion. Failure can be tough, but beating yourself up over it will only hinder your progress. Treat yourself with kindness and understanding. Acknowledge that failure is a natural part of the entrepreneurial journey and that you are doing your best to learn and improve.

In conclusion, building confidence in the face of failure is essential for entrepreneurs, especially beginners who are navigating the challenges of starting a business. By reframing failure, adopting a growth mindset, seeking support, taking small steps, and practicing self-compassion, you can build the resilience and confidence needed to overcome failure and ultimately achieve success. Embrace failure as an opportunity for growth, and you will unlock your full potential as an entrepreneur.

Chapter 6: Failure as Feedback

Viewing Failure as Feedback Rather Than Defeat

Viewing Failure as Feedback Rather Than Defeat

Failure is an inevitable part of the entrepreneurial journey, especially when it comes to starting a business. Many entrepreneurs, beginners in particular, tend to view failure as a defeat rather than an opportunity for growth. However, adopting a mindset that sees failure as feedback can transform the way you approach challenges and setbacks, ultimately leading you towards success.

In the book "Fail Forward: Embracing Failure as an Entrepreneur," we delve into the importance of reframing failure as a valuable learning experience rather than a sign of incompetence. By shifting your perspective, you can harness the power of failure to fuel your personal and professional growth.

One of the key principles to remember is that failure does not define you as an entrepreneur. Instead, it provides feedback on your strategies, decision-making, and areas that require improvement. By embracing failure as feedback, you can identify the specific areas that need adjustment and make informed decisions to pivot or iterate your business model.

Moreover, viewing failure as feedback allows you to detach your self-worth from the outcome of your endeavors. Instead of internalizing failure as a personal flaw, you can separate yourself from the results and focus on the lessons it brings. This mindset shift enables you to maintain a resilient attitude, bounce back from setbacks, and persist in the face of adversity.

Additionally, failure as feedback promotes a culture of continuous learning and innovation. Entrepreneurs who view failure as defeat often shy away from taking risks, fearing the potential consequences. However, those who embrace failure as feedback recognize that each setback is an opportunity to gather insights, make improvements, and ultimately achieve greater success.

To fully leverage failure as feedback, it is crucial to develop a growth mindset. This involves cultivating a belief in your ability to learn, adapt, and overcome challenges. By nurturing a growth mindset, you can embrace failure as an essential part of the entrepreneurial journey, recognizing that setbacks are stepping stones to progress. Let's talk about Jeff, Jeff is a software developer working on a complex coding project. While working on a critical feature, Jeff encounters a series of failures and bugs that prevent the code from functioning as intended. Instead of becoming discouraged, Jeff chooses to view these failures as valuable feedback.

By understanding the specific points of failure, Jeff gains insight into what needs improvement. Identifying Areas for Improvement: Based on the analysis, Jeff identifies specific areas where their code or approach may be lacking. They recognize patterns or common mistakes that contributed to the failures. This allows Jeff to pinpoint the aspects that need refinement and optimization.

To address the areas for improvement, Jeff engages in continuous learning and research. They dive into relevant documentation, tutorials, and forums to expand their knowledge of the specific concepts or techniques related to the failures they encountered.

By seeking out resources and learning from others, Jeff gains new insights and strategies to overcome challenges.

Armed with feedback from failures, Jeff adopts an iterative development approach. They make incremental changes to the code, testing each modification thoroughly. By implementing small adjustments and conducting frequent tests, Jeff can assess the impact of each change and identify potential improvements.

Jeff recognizes the value of collaboration and seeks input from colleagues or fellow developers. They discuss the failures they faced, sharing insights and brainstorming potential solutions together. By leveraging the collective knowledge and experience of their peers, Jeff gains alternative perspectives and discovers new approaches to problem-solving.

To prevent similar failures in the future, Jeff establishes a robust testing framework. They develop comprehensive test cases and conduct thorough testing at various stages of the development process. By implementing effective testing practices, Alex can catch issues early on and validate the code's functionality before it reaches production.

Throughout the journey, Jeff celebrates the progress made. Instead of focusing solely on the failures, they acknowledge and appreciate the lessons learned and improvements achieved along the way.

This positive reinforcement keeps Jeff motivated and confident in their ability to learn from failures and grow as a developer.

By embracing failures as valuable feedback, Jeff transforms setbacks into opportunities for growth and improvement.

Through analysis, learning, collaboration, and iterative development, Jeff's skills and code quality evolve. With each failure encountered, Jeff becomes a more skilled and resilient software developer, equipped with the knowledge and experience to tackle complex challenges successfully.

In conclusion, the subchapter "Viewing Failure as Feedback Rather Than Defeat" emphasizes the importance of reframing failure as an opportunity for growth and improvement. By adopting this mindset, entrepreneurs, especially beginners facing failure in starting a business, can leverage setbacks to their advantage. Failure provides valuable feedback, separates self-worth from outcomes, fosters a culture of learning, and promotes a growth mindset. Ultimately, by viewing failure as feedback, entrepreneurs can navigate the challenges of starting a business with resilience, innovation, and the determination to fail forward.

Utilizing Failure to Improve Decision Making

Utilizing Failure to Improve Decision Making

One of the most common fears among entrepreneurs, especially beginners, is the fear of failure. The thought of investing time, money, and energy into a business venture only to see it fail is enough to discourage even the most ambitious individuals. However, what if failure could be seen as a valuable learning experience rather than a setback? In this subchapter, we will explore the concept of utilizing failure to improve decision making and how it can be a powerful tool for entrepreneurs, especially those facing challenges in starting a business.

Failure is often viewed as something negative, something to be avoided at all costs. But what if we shift our perspective and see failure as an opportunity for growth and improvement? Each failure is a chance to learn valuable lessons, gain experience, and refine our decision-making skills. By embracing failure and analyzing the reasons behind it, entrepreneurs can make better-informed choices in the future.

One key aspect of utilizing failure is the ability to reflect on past decisions. Entrepreneurs should take the time to evaluate what went wrong, what factors contributed to the failure, and what could have been done differently. This process of self-reflection helps to identify patterns, weaknesses, and blind spots that may have been overlooked initially. By acknowledging these areas for improvement, entrepreneurs can make more informed decisions moving forward.

Moreover, failure in starting a business can often provide a reality check. It forces entrepreneurs to question their assumptions and reevaluate their strategies. By examining the causes of failure, entrepreneurs can identify areas where they need to pivot or make adjustments. Failure can act as a catalyst for innovation and creativity, pushing entrepreneurs to come up with new ideas and approaches that may lead to success in the future.

Another way to utilize failure is by seeking feedback and advice from others. Entrepreneurs should not be afraid to reach out to mentors, industry experts, or fellow entrepreneurs who have experienced similar failures. Sharing experiences and learning from others can provide valuable insights and alternative perspectives. This collaborative approach can help entrepreneurs make more informed decisions and avoid repeating the same mistakes.

In conclusion, failure should not be viewed as the end of the road for entrepreneurs, especially those facing challenges in starting a business. Instead, it should be embraced as a stepping stone towards success. By utilizing failure to improve decision making, entrepreneurs can learn from their mistakes, reflect on their decisions, and make better-informed choices in the future. Failure, when approached with the right mindset, can become a powerful tool for growth and innovation. So, don't be afraid to fail, but rather, fail forward and use each setback as a valuable opportunity to improve and achieve entrepreneurial success.

Adapting Strategies Based on Failure

Adapting Strategies Based on Failure

Failure is often viewed as a setback, a roadblock on the path to success. However, as entrepreneurs, it is crucial to recognize failure as an opportunity for growth and learning. In the subchapter "Adapting Strategies Based on Failure," we will delve into the importance of embracing failure and how it can lead to new and improved strategies for starting a business.

Starting a business is no easy task, and many entrepreneurs face failure at some point in their journey. Whether it is a failed product launch, a marketing strategy that didn't resonate with customers, or a missed opportunity, failure is an inevitable part of entrepreneurship. However, what sets successful entrepreneurs apart is their ability to adapt and learn from these failures.

Adapting strategies based on failure involves a shift in mindset. Instead of viewing failure as a personal flaw or a reason to give up, entrepreneurs should see it as a valuable learning experience. By analyzing what went wrong, entrepreneurs can gain insights into their strengths and weaknesses, as well as the market's demands and trends.

One key aspect of adapting strategies based on failure is the ability to pivot. When an initial approach fails, entrepreneurs must be willing to change their course of action. This might involve tweaking their product or service, redefining their target audience, or exploring new marketing channels. By adapting their strategies, entrepreneurs can align their business more effectively with market needs and increase their chances of success.

Furthermore, failure can also spark innovation. When faced with failure, entrepreneurs are often forced to think outside the box and come up with creative solutions. This may involve exploring alternative business models, embracing emerging technologies, or seeking partnerships. By adapting their strategies based on failure, entrepreneurs can unlock new opportunities and differentiate themselves in the market.

To successfully adapt strategies based on failure, entrepreneurs should cultivate a growth mindset. This involves embracing challenges, persisting in the face of setbacks, and seeking feedback and mentorship. By surrounding themselves with a support network of experienced entrepreneurs and industry experts, beginners can gain valuable insights and perspectives that will help them adapt their strategies effectively.

In conclusion, failure should not be feared but embraced as a stepping stone to success. By adapting strategies based on failure, entrepreneurs can turn setbacks into opportunities for growth and improvement. Through a shift in mindset, a willingness to pivot, and a commitment to innovation, entrepreneurs can navigate the challenges of starting a business and increase their chances of long-term success.

Chapter 7: Embracing Failure as a Learning Process

The Importance of Experimentation and Iteration

The Importance of Experimentation and Iteration

In the journey of entrepreneurship, failure is not just an option – it is an essential stepping stone towards success. As entrepreneurs, beginners often feel apprehensive about failure, fearing it will tarnish their reputation or undermine their dreams. However, it is crucial to understand that failure is not the end of the road, but rather an opportunity for growth and learning. One of the most effective ways to embrace failure and turn it into a catalyst for success is through experimentation and iteration.

When starting a business, failure is almost inevitable. The road to success is paved with obstacles, challenges, and setbacks. However, what separates successful entrepreneurs from the rest is their ability to embrace failure and use it as a valuable learning experience. Experimentation allows entrepreneurs to test their assumptions, products, and strategies in a controlled environment. By conducting experiments, entrepreneurs can gather vital data and insights, enabling them to make informed decisions and refine their approach.

The beauty of experimentation lies in its ability to provide entrepreneurs with real-world feedback. Rather than relying solely on assumptions and guesswork, experimentation allows entrepreneurs to collect concrete evidence about what works and what doesn't. This data-driven approach minimizes the risk of failure and increases the chances of success. It provides entrepreneurs with the opportunity to pivot, adapt, and refine their business model, ensuring they are always moving in the right direction.

However, experimentation alone is not enough. The key to success lies in iteration – the process of continuously refining and improving upon previous versions. Entrepreneurs must be willing to iterate, to tweak and adjust their strategies based on the lessons learned from experimentation. This iterative process allows entrepreneurs to adapt to changing circumstances, customer feedback, and market demands. It ensures that entrepreneurs are constantly evolving, staying ahead of the competition, and delivering exceptional value to their customers.

In the realm of failure in starting a business, experimentation and iteration are not just important – they are essential. They provide entrepreneurs with the tools to navigate the challenges of entrepreneurship, learn from their failures, and ultimately achieve success. By embracing failure as a necessary part of the journey, entrepreneurs can unlock their true potential and turn their dreams into reality. So, let go of the fear of failure, embrace experimentation, and iterate your way towards the entrepreneurial success you desire.

Embracing Failure as a Stepping Stone to Success

Embracing Failure as a Stepping Stone to Success

Introduction:
Starting a business is a daunting task, filled with risks and uncertainties. Many entrepreneurs often find themselves facing failure in their early stages, and it can be disheartening. However, failure should not be seen as the end of the road but rather as a stepping stone to success. In this subchapter, we will explore the concept of embracing failure and how it can propel entrepreneurs forward in their journey towards success.

Understanding Failure:
Failure is an inevitable part of the entrepreneurial journey. It is important to understand that failure does not define you as an entrepreneur, but rather serves as a learning experience. Each setback provides valuable lessons that

can be utilized to improve and grow both personally and professionally. Embracing failure requires a shift in mindset, from viewing it as a negative experience to seeing it as an opportunity for growth.

Learning from Failure:
Failure provides an opportunity to reflect on what went wrong and identify areas of improvement. By analyzing the reasons behind the failure, entrepreneurs can gain valuable insights and adjust their strategies accordingly. It is essential to take a proactive approach and use failure as a springboard for innovation and creativity. Embracing failure allows entrepreneurs to develop resilience, adaptability, and a growth mindset.

Overcoming Fear of Failure:
Fear of failure can be a significant barrier to success. Many beginners hesitate to take risks or pursue their entrepreneurial dreams due to the fear of failure. However, it is crucial to acknowledge that failure is a natural part of the journey. By reframing the fear of failure as an opportunity for growth, entrepreneurs can take calculated risks and explore new avenues with confidence. Embracing failure allows entrepreneurs to push their boundaries and discover their true potential.

Celebrating Small Wins:
While failure may be discouraging, it is important to celebrate small wins along the way. Each small success serves as a reminder that progress is being made, even in the face of failure. By acknowledging and celebrating these wins, entrepreneurs can maintain motivation, confidence, and momentum in their entrepreneurial journey.

Conclusion:
Embracing failure as a stepping stone to success is a mindset that all entrepreneurs should adopt. By understanding failure, learning from it, overcoming the fear of failure, and celebrating small wins, entrepreneurs can transform setbacks into opportunities for growth. Failure is not the end but rather a crucial part of the journey towards success. Embrace failure, learn from it, and let it propel you forward as you build the business of your dreams.

Learning from Failure to Improve Business Practices

Subchapter: Learning from Failure to Improve Business Practices

Introduction:
Failure is an inevitable part of entrepreneurship, especially for beginners embarking on their journey to start a business. While it can be disheartening and demoralizing, failure should not be viewed as the end of the road. Instead, it should be seen as an opportunity for growth and improvement. In this subchapter, we will explore the concept of learning from failure to enhance business practices. By embracing failure, entrepreneurs can gain valuable insights and develop strategies to increase their chances of success.

1. Embracing Failure as a Stepping Stone:
One of the key mindsets that entrepreneurs must adopt is to view failure as a stepping stone rather than a stumbling block. By reframing failure as a valuable learning experience, entrepreneurs can identify the areas that need improvement and make necessary adjustments to their business practices.

2. Analyzing the Causes of Failure:
To learn from failure, it is crucial to analyze the root causes of the setback. Was it a lack of market research, ineffective marketing strategies, or poor financial management? By identifying the specific factors that contributed to the failure, entrepreneurs can take corrective actions and prevent similar mistakes in the future.

3. Seeking Feedback and Mentorship:
Entrepreneurs should actively seek feedback from customers, industry experts, and mentors. Constructive criticism can provide valuable insights into areas that require improvement. Additionally, having a mentor who has experienced failure can provide guidance and support, helping entrepreneurs navigate through challenges more effectively.

4. Iterative Approach and Continuous Improvement:
Failure should not discourage entrepreneurs from pursuing their dreams.
Instead, it should encourage them to adopt an iterative approach and focus on
continuous improvement. By embracing a growth mindset and implementing
agile practices, entrepreneurs can adapt and pivot their business strategies
based on the lessons learned from failure.

5. Implementing Fail-Safe Measures:
Learning from failure also involves implementing fail-safe measures to
mitigate risks. This can include conducting thorough market research, creating
contingency plans, and diversifying revenue streams. By taking proactive steps
to anticipate potential failures, entrepreneurs can minimize the impact and
recover more quickly.

Conclusion:
Failure in starting a business is not a sign of incompetence but an opportunity
for growth. By embracing failure and learning from it, entrepreneurs can
improve their business practices, refine their strategies, and increase their
chances of success. Remember, failure is not the end; it is merely a stepping
stone on the path to entrepreneurial greatness. Embrace failure, learn from it,
and let it propel you toward future achievements.

Chapter 8: Developing a Growth Mindset for Resilience

Recognizing the Value of a Growth Mindset

Recognizing the Value of a Growth Mindset

In the realm of entrepreneurship, failure is often viewed as a setback, a roadblock, or even a sign of incompetence. However, in the book "Fail Forward: Embracing Failure as an Entrepreneur," we challenge this conventional thinking and encourage entrepreneurs, especially beginners, to recognize the value of a growth mindset when it comes to failure in starting a business.

A growth mindset is a powerful concept that can transform how we perceive and respond to failure. It is the belief that our abilities and intelligence can be developed through dedication, hard work, and a willingness to learn from our mistakes. This mindset emphasizes the importance of effort, resilience, and continuous improvement.

For entrepreneurs facing failure in starting a business, adopting a growth mindset is crucial. Rather than viewing failure as a personal flaw or a dead end, it becomes an opportunity for growth and learning. Instead of giving up, entrepreneurs with a growth mindset embrace failure as a stepping stone towards success.

One key aspect of recognizing the value of a growth mindset is reframing failure as feedback. Every setback, mistake, or misstep provides valuable information that can guide future decisions and strategies. By analyzing what went wrong, entrepreneurs can identify areas for improvement, refine their approaches, and ultimately increase their chances of success.

Moreover, a growth mindset encourages entrepreneurs to embrace challenges and push beyond their comfort zones. Starting a business is a risky endeavor, and setbacks are bound to happen. However, with a growth mindset, entrepreneurs perceive these challenges as opportunities for personal and professional development. They understand that failure is not a reflection of their abilities, but rather a necessary part of the journey towards success.

To cultivate a growth mindset, entrepreneurs can engage in various practices. Continuous learning, seeking feedback from mentors and peers, and embracing failure as a natural part of the entrepreneurial journey are all essential steps. By reframing failure, developing resilience, and maintaining a forward-thinking perspective, entrepreneurs can harness the power of a growth mindset to overcome obstacles and achieve their goals.

In conclusion, recognizing the value of a growth mindset is crucial for entrepreneurs, especially beginners, facing failure in starting a business. By embracing failure as an opportunity for growth and learning, reframing setbacks as feedback, and adopting a forward-thinking perspective, entrepreneurs can navigate the challenges of entrepreneurship with resilience and determination. With a growth mindset, failure becomes a stepping stone towards success, rather than a roadblock.

Nurturing a Growth Mindset in the Face of Failure

Nurturing a Growth Mindset in the Face of Failure

Failure is often seen as a setback, a roadblock on the path to success. However, what if we were to tell you that failure is not the opposite of success, but rather a stepping stone towards it? In the world of entrepreneurship, failure is not only common but also necessary for growth and innovation. This chapter aims to explore the concept of nurturing a growth mindset in the face of failure, specifically in the context of starting a business.

As entrepreneurs and beginners in the business world, it is crucial to recognize that failure is not the end of the road. It is merely a detour that guides us towards a better understanding of ourselves, our ideas, and the market. Embracing failure as a valuable learning experience is the key to cultivating a growth mindset.

One of the first steps in nurturing a growth mindset is reframing our perception of failure. Rather than seeing it as a personal flaw or a sign of incompetence, we must view failure as an opportunity to learn, adapt, and improve. Failure should be embraced as a natural part of the entrepreneurial journey, where setbacks are transformed into valuable lessons that pave the way for future success.

Another crucial aspect of nurturing a growth mindset in the face of failure is developing resilience. Entrepreneurs must bounce back from failure with determination and perseverance. This resilience can be cultivated by focusing on the lessons learned, seeking feedback, and continuously improving upon our failures. It involves developing a mindset that sees failure not as a final destination but as a stepping stone towards growth and achievement.

Furthermore, entrepreneurs should surround themselves with a supportive network of like-minded individuals who understand the challenges of starting a business. Sharing experiences, insights, and failures with others can provide valuable perspective and encouragement. This network can also serve as a source of inspiration, motivation, and guidance during difficult times.

In conclusion, nurturing a growth mindset in the face of failure is a critical skill for entrepreneurs and beginners in the business world. By reframing our perception of failure, developing resilience, and building a supportive network, we can transform setbacks into opportunities for growth and success.

Embracing failure as an integral part of the entrepreneurial journey allows us to learn, adapt, and ultimately thrive in the face of adversity.

Strategies for Cultivating Resilience

Strategies for Cultivating Resilience

Resilience is a crucial quality that every entrepreneur needs to develop in order to navigate the challenging journey of starting a business. It is the ability to bounce back from failures, setbacks, and disappointments, and continue moving forward with renewed determination. In this subchapter, we will explore effective strategies for cultivating resilience, ensuring that failure becomes a stepping stone rather than a stumbling block on your entrepreneurial path.

1. Embrace a Growth Mindset: Adopting a growth mindset is vital for building resilience. Understand that failure is not a reflection of your worth or abilities, but an opportunity to learn, grow, and improve. Embrace challenges as a chance to stretch your capabilities and view setbacks as valuable feedback.

2. Seek Support: Surround yourself with a network of like-minded individuals who understand the challenges of starting a business and are willing to provide support. Join relevant communities, attend networking events, and seek mentors who can offer guidance and encouragement during tough times. Having a support system can help you regain perspective and keep moving forward.

3. Practice Self-Care: Entrepreneurship can be demanding, both mentally and physically. Taking care of yourself is essential for cultivating resilience. Prioritize self-care activities such as exercise, meditation, journaling, and spending time with loved ones. It is crucial to recharge your batteries regularly to maintain focus and resilience.

4. Learn from Failure: Instead of dwelling on failures, learn from them. Analyze what went wrong, identify areas for improvement, and develop strategies to avoid similar mistakes in the future. Adopt a growth mindset that embraces failure as an opportunity to gain valuable insights and refine your business strategies.

5. Set Realistic Goals: Setting realistic goals helps manage expectations and avoid unnecessary stress. Break down your long-term goals into smaller, attainable milestones. Celebrate each achievement along the way, as this not only provides motivation but also strengthens your resilience.

6. Stay Flexible: The entrepreneurial journey is rarely a straight path. Be prepared to adapt and pivot when necessary. Embrace the mindset of continuous learning and remain open to new ideas and opportunities. This flexibility will allow you to navigate unexpected challenges and setbacks with resilience.

In conclusion, cultivating resilience is essential for entrepreneurs, especially when faced with failures in starting a business. Developing a growth mindset, seeking support, practicing self-care, learning from failure, setting realistic goals, and staying flexible are all effective strategies that will help you bounce back stronger and continue moving forward. Remember, failure is not the end; it is a stepping stone towards success. Embrace failure, learn from it, and keep moving forward on your entrepreneurial journey.

Chapter 9: Overcoming Setbacks and Bouncing Back

Dealing with Setbacks and Disappointments

Dealing with Setbacks and Disappointments

In the journey of entrepreneurship, setbacks and disappointments are inevitable. Starting a business is a challenging endeavor, and it's important to develop resilience and embrace failure as a stepping stone towards success. This subchapter aims to provide valuable insights and strategies on how to effectively deal with setbacks and disappointments in your entrepreneurial journey.

1. Embrace Failure as a Learning Opportunity:

Failure is not the end; it's an opportunity for growth. Instead of dwelling on setbacks and disappointments, view them as learning experiences that can propel you forward. Analyze what went wrong, identify the lessons learned, and use that knowledge to improve your future endeavors.

2. Cultivate a Growth Mindset:

A growth mindset is essential when facing setbacks and disappointments. Understand that challenges are a part of the entrepreneurial journey, and setbacks are not indicative of your abilities or potential. Embrace the belief that you have the ability to learn, adapt, and overcome any obstacle that comes your way.

3. Seek Support:

Entrepreneurship can be a lonely path, especially when faced with setbacks. Surround yourself with a supportive network of mentors, fellow entrepreneurs, or industry experts who can provide guidance and encouragement during challenging times. Their insights and experiences can help you gain perspective and find innovative solutions to overcome setbacks.

4. Practice Resilience:

Resilience is the key to bouncing back from setbacks. Develop coping mechanisms to help you navigate through disappointments. Maintain a positive mindset, practice self-care, and engage in activities that rejuvenate your spirit. Remember that setbacks are temporary roadblocks, and with resilience, you can overcome them. I usually post inspirational quotes like these Motivational quotes for entrepreneurs
"All our dreams can come true if we have the courage to pursue them." — Walt Disney "
The secret of getting ahead is getting started." —Mark Twain
"I've missed more than 9,000 shots in my career. I've lost almost 300 games. 26 times I've been trusted to take the game-winning shot and missed. I've failed over and over and over again in my life, and that is why I succeed." — Michael Jordan
"Don't limit yourself. Many people limit themselves to what they think they can do. You can go as far as your mind lets you. What you believe, remember, you can achieve." —Mary Kay Ash
"The best time to plant a tree was 20 years ago. The second best time is now." —Chinese Proverb
"Only the paranoid survive." —Andy Grove
"It's hard to beat a person who never gives up." —Babe Ruth
"I wake up every morning and think to myself, 'How far can I push this company in the next 24 hours.'" —Leah Busque
"If people are doubting how far you can go, go so far that you can't hear them anymore.

" —Michele Ruiz
"We need to accept that we won't always make the right decisions, that we'll

screw up royally sometimes understanding that failure is not the opposite of success, it's part of success." —Arianna Huffington

5. Adapt and Pivot:

When faced with setbacks, be willing to adapt and pivot your business strategy. Evaluate your approach, identify areas that require improvement, and be open to making necessary changes. Successful entrepreneurs understand the importance of being flexible and adjusting their plans when needed, ultimately turning setbacks into opportunities.

Conclusion:

Dealing with setbacks and disappointments is an integral part of the entrepreneurial journey. By embracing failure as a learning opportunity, cultivating a growth mindset, seeking support, practicing resilience, and adapting when necessary, you can transform setbacks into stepping stones towards success. Remember, failure is not the end, but rather a catalyst for growth and innovation. Embrace it, learn from it, and continue to persevere on your path to entrepreneurial success.

Building Resilience to Overcome Failure

Building Resilience to Overcome Failure

Failure is an inevitable part of any entrepreneurial journey, especially during the initial stages of starting a business. It is crucial for entrepreneurs, especially beginners, to develop resilience in order to overcome these setbacks and continue on the path to success. In this subchapter, we will explore various strategies and mindsets that can help you build resilience and embrace failure as an entrepreneur.

The first step towards building resilience is changing your perspective on failure. Rather than viewing failure as a negative outcome, see it as a valuable learning experience. Every failure is an opportunity to grow, learn, and improve. Embrace failure as a stepping stone towards success, knowing that each setback brings you one step closer to achieving your goals.

Another important aspect of building resilience is developing a growth mindset. Understand that your abilities and skills are not fixed, but can be developed through dedication and effort. Embrace challenges and setbacks as opportunities to expand your knowledge and skills. Seek feedback and learn from your mistakes, continuously striving for improvement.

Resilient entrepreneurs also understand the importance of self-care and maintaining a positive mindset. Taking care of your physical and mental well-being is essential for bouncing back from failures. Engage in activities that help you relax and recharge, such as exercise, meditation, or spending time with loved ones. Surround yourself with a support network of like-minded individuals who can provide encouragement and guidance during tough times.

Additionally, it is important to develop a problem-solving mindset. Rather than dwelling on the failure itself, focus on finding solutions and taking action. Analyze the reasons behind the failure, identify areas for improvement, and adapt your strategies accordingly. Embrace a flexible and adaptable approach to problem-solving, as this will help you navigate the challenges that arise along the way.

Finally, celebrate small wins and milestones on your entrepreneurial journey. Recognize and appreciate the progress you have made, regardless of the outcome. By acknowledging your achievements, you build confidence and motivation to keep moving forward, even in the face of failure.

In conclusion, building resilience is essential for entrepreneurs, especially beginners, who may face failure in starting their business. By changing your perspective on failure, developing a growth mindset, practicing self-care, adopting a problem-solving approach, and celebrating small wins, you can overcome setbacks and continue on the path to success. Embrace failure as a valuable learning experience, and remember that resilience is the key to turning failure into a stepping stone towards achieving your entrepreneurial goals.

Strategies for Bouncing Back Stronger

Strategies for Bouncing Back Stronger

Failure is an inevitable part of the entrepreneurial journey, especially when it comes to starting a business. However, it is how we respond to failure that truly defines our success. In this subchapter, we will explore strategies that can help entrepreneurs bounce back stronger from failures and embrace them as learning opportunities.

1. Embrace a Growth Mindset: Adopting a growth mindset is crucial for entrepreneurs who have experienced failure in starting a business. Instead of viewing failure as a setback, see it as an opportunity for growth and

improvement. Understand that failure is not a reflection of your abilities, but rather a stepping stone towards success.

2. Learn from Mistakes: Take the time to analyze and understand the reasons behind your failures. Reflect on what went wrong, identify the mistakes you made, and learn from them. This self-reflection process will enable you to avoid making similar mistakes in the future and make better-informed decisions.

3. Seek Support: Surround yourself with a network of like-minded individuals who can provide support and guidance during challenging times. Join entrepreneurship communities, attend networking events, and seek mentorship from experienced entrepreneurs who have overcome failures themselves. Their insights and encouragement can help you gain perspective and find creative solutions.

4. Pivot and Adapt: Sometimes, failures occur because the initial business idea or strategy is not working as expected. In such cases, it is important to be open to change and willing to pivot your approach. Adaptability is key in the entrepreneurial world, and by being flexible and open-minded, you can turn a failure into an opportunity for innovation.

5. Stay Persistent: Failure can be discouraging, but it is essential to stay persistent and not give up. Remember that many successful entrepreneurs have faced numerous failures before finding their breakthrough. Use failure as motivation to keep pushing forward, learning from each setback, and refining your strategies.

6. Celebrate Small Wins: Along your entrepreneurial journey, celebrate the small wins to boost your confidence and maintain a positive mindset. Recognize that failure is not the end but rather a stepping stone towards success. By acknowledging your progress, you will build resilience and maintain the determination to overcome future obstacles.

In conclusion, failure in starting a business is not a sign of defeat but an opportunity for growth. By embracing a growth mindset, learning from mistakes, seeking support, pivoting and adapting, staying persistent, and celebrating small wins, entrepreneurs can bounce back stronger from failures and ultimately achieve success. Remember, failure is not the end, but merely a stepping stone on the path to greatness.

Chapter 10: Embracing Failure as an Entrepreneur

The Journey of Successful Entrepreneurs

The Journey of Successful Entrepreneurs

In the exhilarating world of entrepreneurship, success is often portrayed as the ultimate destination. We hear stories of overnight triumphs and multi-million-dollar acquisitions, leaving us in awe and wondering how these individuals achieved such incredible feats. However, what these stories often fail to mention is the arduous journey of challenges, setbacks, and failures that these successful entrepreneurs have endured.

This subchapter, titled "The Journey of Successful Entrepreneurs," aims to shed light on the untold stories behind their triumphs. It serves as a reminder to aspiring entrepreneurs that failure is an integral part of the process and should be embraced rather than feared.

For beginners entering the business world, failure can be a daunting prospect. The fear of failure often paralyzes individuals, preventing them from taking the necessary risks and exploring their potential. However, successful entrepreneurs understand that failure is merely a stepping stone towards success. They have experienced countless setbacks, learned from their mistakes, and used these failures as opportunities for growth.

One crucial aspect of the journey of successful entrepreneurs is their ability to adapt and pivot. Starting a business is a risky endeavor, and unforeseen challenges are bound to arise. These entrepreneurs possess the resilience and flexibility to adjust their strategies and navigate through uncharted territories. They are not deterred by failures; instead, they view them as valuable lessons that allow them to refine their ideas and approaches.

Another characteristic of successful entrepreneurs is their unwavering determination. They possess a burning passion for their vision, which fuels their perseverance during the most challenging times. They understand that setbacks are not indicative of their worth or potential but rather temporary obstacles in their path to success.

Moreover, successful entrepreneurs surround themselves with a supportive network. They seek guidance from mentors, collaborate with like-minded individuals, and build a team that complements their skillset. These relationships provide emotional support, guidance, and valuable insights that contribute to their growth and success.

For entrepreneurs who have experienced failure in starting a business, this subchapter serves as a beacon of hope and inspiration. It encourages them to reframe their perspective, viewing failure not as a dead-end but as an opportunity for personal and professional development. It highlights that failure is not exclusive to beginners but an inherent part of the entrepreneurial journey.

In conclusion, the journey of successful entrepreneurs is riddled with failures and setbacks. However, it is their ability to embrace failure, adapt to challenges, maintain determination, and build supportive networks that ultimately leads them to triumph. This subchapter serves as a guide for entrepreneurs, beginners, and those who have faced failures in starting a business, reminding them that failure is not the end but a stepping stone towards greatness.

Embracing Failure as an Inevitable Part of Entrepreneurship

Embracing Failure as an Inevitable Part of Entrepreneurship

Failure is often viewed as a negative outcome, something to be avoided at all costs. However, in the world of entrepreneurship, failure is not only expected but also celebrated as a stepping stone towards success. Embracing failure as an inevitable part of entrepreneurship is crucial for aspiring entrepreneurs, especially beginners who often find themselves overwhelmed by the challenges of starting a business.

Starting a business is a risky endeavor, and failure is an inherent part of that risk. Many successful entrepreneurs have experienced multiple failures before achieving their breakthrough. It is these failures that provide valuable lessons and insights, shaping their future success. Failure should be seen as a learning opportunity rather than a setback, a chance to identify areas for improvement and make necessary adjustments.

One of the main reasons failure is so prevalent in starting a business is the unpredictable nature of the market. Entrepreneurs often have to navigate uncharted territory, facing countless unknowns along the way. It is impossible to predict every outcome or foresee every obstacle. Embracing failure means acknowledging these uncertainties and being prepared to adapt and pivot when necessary.

Failure also forces entrepreneurs to confront their weaknesses and limitations. It pushes them out of their comfort zones, encouraging personal and professional growth. By embracing failure, entrepreneurs develop resilience, perseverance, and the ability to bounce back from setbacks. These qualities are invaluable in the entrepreneurial journey and are often the differentiating factor between success and failure.

Furthermore, failure can be a source of inspiration and motivation. Many successful entrepreneurs have shared stories of how their failures fueled their determination to succeed. Failure forces entrepreneurs to reassess their goals, refine their strategies, and ultimately become more innovative. It breeds creativity and encourages out-of-the-box thinking, pushing entrepreneurs to find new solutions to old problems.

Embracing failure is not about seeking failure or celebrating it for its own sake. Instead, it is about understanding that failure is a natural part of the entrepreneurial process. It is about learning from failure, adapting, and persevering. By embracing failure, entrepreneurs can turn setbacks into stepping stones, paving the way for future success.

In conclusion, failure in starting a business is inevitable, but it should not be feared or avoided. Embracing failure as an inevitable part of entrepreneurship is essential for entrepreneurs, especially beginners. It provides valuable lessons, fosters personal and professional growth, and fuels innovation. By embracing failure, entrepreneurs can develop resilience and perseverance, ultimately increasing their chances of success in the entrepreneurial journey.

Celebrating Failures and Building Success

Subchapter: Celebrating Failures and Building Success

Introduction:
In the journey of entrepreneurship, failures are inevitable. However, what sets successful entrepreneurs apart is their ability to embrace failure, learn from it, and use it as a stepping stone towards achieving their goals. In this subchapter, we will explore the concept of celebrating failures and how it can help you build success in your entrepreneurial endeavors.

1. The Importance of Failure:
Failure is not the end; it is merely a stepping stone towards success. It provides valuable lessons, insights, and an opportunity for growth. Understanding the significance of failure and embracing it as a part of your entrepreneurial journey is crucial for long-term success.

2. Changing the Perception of Failure:
Many entrepreneurs fear failure and view it as something negative. However, by shifting your perspective and seeing failure as a learning experience, you can change the way you approach challenges. Celebrating failures means

reframing them as valuable lessons, acknowledging your efforts, and appreciating the courage it takes to step out of your comfort zone.

3. Learning from Failures:

Failures provide an opportunity to evaluate what went wrong, identify areas for improvement, and refine your strategies. By analyzing your failures, you can gain valuable insights into your business model, market trends, customer preferences, and your own strengths and weaknesses. This knowledge will help you make informed decisions and avoid repeating the same mistakes in the future.

4. Cultivating Resilience and Perseverance:

Celebrating failures helps entrepreneurs develop resilience and perseverance. It enables you to bounce back stronger, learn from setbacks, and continue pursuing your dreams. By embracing failure, you become more adaptable, tenacious, and better equipped to handle the challenges that come your way.

5. Creating a Supportive Network:

Entrepreneurship can be a lonely journey, especially when faced with failures. Surrounding yourself with like-minded individuals who understand and support your journey is crucial. By building a network of fellow entrepreneurs, mentors, and advisors, you can share experiences, learn from each other's failures, and gain valuable insights that can contribute to your success.

Conclusion:

Failures are not the enemy; they are your greatest teachers. By celebrating failures, you can unlock the door to success. Embrace the lessons learned, adapt your strategies, and continue moving forward with resilience and determination. Remember, failure is not the end; it is a stepping stone towards building your entrepreneurial success.

Conclusion: Embracing Failure as a Catalyst for Growth

Conclusion: Embracing Failure as a Catalyst for Growth

In the journey of entrepreneurship, failure is often seen as a dreaded outcome, something to be avoided at all costs. However, what if I told you that failure could actually be a catalyst for growth? This may sound counterintuitive, but the truth is that failure holds immense potential for learning, innovation, and personal development.

For entrepreneurs, especially beginners, failure in starting a business is a common occurrence. It can be disheartening and demoralizing, causing many to question their abilities and even contemplate giving up. But it is during these moments of failure that we have a unique opportunity to reflect, reassess, and pivot towards a better path.

One of the most important lessons that failure teaches us is resilience. When we experience setbacks and challenges, we are forced to dig deep within ourselves to find the strength and determination to keep going. The ability to bounce back from failure is an invaluable trait that separates successful entrepreneurs from the rest. Embracing failure as a catalyst for growth means understanding that setbacks are not the end, but rather valuable stepping stones on the road to success.

Failure also provides us with invaluable feedback. When something doesn't go as planned, it is an opportunity to analyze what went wrong and identify areas for improvement. By understanding the root causes of failure, we can make informed decisions, refine our strategies, and implement necessary changes to increase our chances of success in the future.

Moreover, failure often pushes us out of our comfort zones and encourages us to think outside the box. It forces us to challenge our assumptions, experiment with new ideas, and innovate. Some of the greatest inventions and breakthroughs in history have been the result of multiple failures. Embracing failure as a catalyst for growth means embracing the unknown, taking risks, and pushing the boundaries of what is possible.

Ultimately, failure is not an indicator of our worth or potential. It is merely a stepping stone on the path to success. By reframing our mindset and embracing failure as an opportunity for growth, we can transform setbacks into stepping stones, failures into lessons, and ultimately, our dreams into reality.

So, fellow entrepreneurs, beginners or seasoned, let us not fear failure, but rather embrace it. Let us learn from our mistakes, adapt our strategies, and keep moving forward. Failure is not the end; it is just the beginning of a new chapter in our entrepreneurial journey. Embrace failure, and watch as it becomes the catalyst for your growth and success.

www.ingramcontent.com/pod-product-compliance
Lightning Source LLC
Chambersburg PA
CBHW062243290526
45794CB00006B/2382